W9-APV-043

Make Way for the King of the Jungle

Other Peanuts Books from Andrews and McMeel

Dr. Snoopy's Advice to Pet Owners

Being a Dog Is a Full-Time Job

Around the World in 45 Years: Charlie Brown's Anniversary Celebration

Make Way for the King of the Jungle

A Peanuts® Collection

by Charles M. Schulz

Andrews and McMeel
A Universal Press Syndicate Company
Kansas City

Make Way for the King of the Jungle copyright © 1995 United Feature Syndicate, Inc. All rights reserved. PEANUTS Comic Strips © 1989 and 1990 United Feature Syndicate, Inc. Printed in the United States of America. No part of this book may be used or reproduced in any manner whatsoever without written permission except in the case of reviews. For information write to Andrews and McMeel, a Universal Press Syndicate Company, 4520 Main Street, Kansas City Missouri 64111.

ISBN: 0-8362-1788-8

Library of Congress Catalog Card Number: 94-73237

00 01 BAH 10 9 8 7

—— **ATTENTION: SCHOOLS AND BUSINESSES** ——

Andrews and McMeel books are available at quantity discounts for bulk purchase for educational, business, or sales promotional use. For information, please write to Special Sales Department, Andrews and McMeel, 4520 Main Street, Kansas City, Missouri 64111.

5

7

YEAH, CHUCK, I'M CALLING YOU BECAUSE I NEED SOMEBODY TO PLAY FOOTBALL WITH... MARCIE IS JUST TOO WEIRD...

ASK HIM IF HE STILL LOVES ME

SO LONG, CHUCK

YOU DIDN'T ASK HIM

HE NEVER WOULD HAVE UNDERSTOOD THE QUESTION, MARCIE

THANKS FOR COMING, GUYS..

I'M GLAD SOMEBODY IS STILL INTERESTED IN PLAYING FOOTBALL..

JUST TRY NEVER TO BRING UP THE SUBJECT OF KNEE SURGERY..

WELL! I'M GLAD TO SEE YOU'RE WATCHING THE NEWS... WHAT'S GOING ON IN THE WORLD?

THE ANCHOR PERSON LOOKED BETTER WHEN SHE HAD LONG HAIR..

STOP SAYING, "PLAY IT AGAIN, SAM"!

I GUESS YOU CAN NEVER COUNT ON THE WEATHER..

WHEN WE LEFT, IT WAS NICE AND CLEAR..NOW, LOOK WHAT WE'RE RUNNING INTO...

COASTAL FOG!

MY GRAMPA AND GRAMMA HAVE BEEN MARRIED FOR FIFTY YEARS...

THEY'RE LUCKY, AREN'T THEY?

GRAMPA SAYS IT ISN'T LUCK.. IT'S SKILL!

I THINK WHAT HAPPENS IS THAT SOMETIMES HE JUST GETS TIRED OF EATING ALONE..

YES, MA'AM..WELL, I'LL GUESS..I MEAN, I'LL SAY, "GUATEMALA"

I WAS RIGHT? WELL, I'LL BE!

NO CAMERAS, PLEASE!

HERE'S THE WORLD WAR I FLYING ACE DRINKING ROOT BEER IN A SMALL CAFE IN FRANCE..HE IS DEPRESSED...

THE WAR DRAGS ON ..IT ALL SEEMS HOPELESS..HE LONGS FOR SOMEONE TO TALK TO.. SOMEONE WHO WILL UNDERSTAND..

MOM..

HERE'S THE WORLD WAR I FLYING ACE SITTING NEXT TO A BEAUTIFUL FRENCH LASS

HE MUST THINK OF SOME WAY TO GET HER ATTENTION...

WOULD MADEMOISELLE CARE FOR ONE-EIGHTH OF A DOUGHNUT?

SO, MONSIEUR..I AM TOLD THAT YOU ARE THE FAMOUS FLYING ACE...

YOU ARE SO FAMOUS THAT THE RED BARON SAYS HE MUST DESTROY YOU!

I'VE NEVER HEARD OF ME..

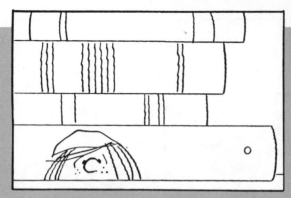

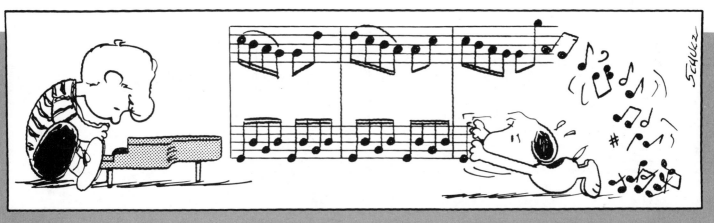

I'VE BEEN HAVING THE STRANGEST DREAMS LATELY..I'M PLAYING THE PIANO, AND ALL THE NOTES KEEP SORT OF FALLING AWAY...

SNOOPY IS THERE, TOO, AND...

MAYBE YOU SHOULD TRY TO DREAM ABOUT **ME**...

THESE ARE DREAMS, NOT NIGHTMARES..

 IT'S HARD TO CONCENTRATE IN SCHOOL WHEN YOU THINK ABOUT YOUR DOG BEING AT HOME ALL ALONE...

 THAT'S WHY I RUSH HOME AS FAST AS I CAN BECAUSE I KNOW HE MISSES ME TOO..

 WHERE ARE THE COOKIES?

RING!

WELL?!

GOOD MORNING.. I'M HERE TO TELL YOU ABOUT THE "GREAT PUMPKIN"

FORGET IT!

SLAM!

GOOD MORNING.. DO YOU REALIZE THAT THE "GREAT PUMPKIN" WILL BE HERE IN ONLY THREE WEEKS?

THAT'S RIGHT.. ON HALLOWEEN NIGHT...

YOU'RE KIND OF CUTE.. COME ON IN...

IF YOU COME IN, I'LL TELL YOU WHY I CAN'T GO OUT..

Dear Great Pumpkin, The first person I talked to today slammed the door in my face.

I think the second person I talked to gave me the chicken pox.

IS IT TRUE THAT YOU'VE BEEN PRACTICING LAW WITH A DOG LICENSE?

IT'S IMPOLITE TO ASK AN ATTORNEY SOMETHING THAT MAKES HIS HAT FLY OFF..

WE'VE BEEN READING POEMS IN SCHOOL, BUT I NEVER UNDERSTAND ANY OF THEM..

HOW AM I SUPPOSED TO KNOW WHICH POEMS TO LIKE?

SOMEBODY TELLS YOU

SOMEDAY, TROOPS, SOMEONE WILL ASK YOU WHY WE CLIMBED THIS MOUNTAIN, AND YOU CAN ANSWER SIMPLY, "BECAUSE IT WAS THERE!"

YES, I SUPPOSE YOU COULD ALSO ADMIT WE HAD NOTHING ELSE TO DO..

I'LL BE THERE AS SOON AS I FEED THE DOG..

BONK!

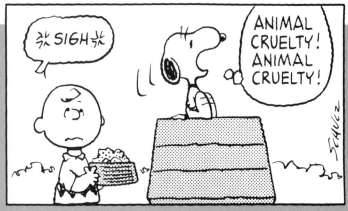

⁂SIGH⁂

ANIMAL CRUELTY! ANIMAL CRUELTY!

ALL I SEEM TO WANT TO DO LATELY IS SIT AROUND HOLDING MY DOG IN MY LAP...

THE DOCTOR IS IN

I'M NOT EVEN SURE WHY HE'S WILLING TO LET ME HOLD HIM...

LOVE AND A SHORT LEASH

WHAT WOULD YOU SAY IF I TOLD YOU I WAS GOING TO DEVOTE THE REST OF MY LIFE TO MAKING YOU HAPPY?

WE'LL GO FOR LONG WALKS IN THE WOODS AND ROMP AROUND IN THE YARD...

YOU'LL SIT IN MY LAP, AND I'LL SCRATCH YOUR EARS, AND WE'LL WATCH TV AND I'LL GIVE YOU COOKIES...

WHAT KIND OF COOKIES?

YES, MA'AM..I'VE DECIDED TO QUIT SCHOOL..I'LL PROBABLY NEVER AMOUNT TO ANYTHING ANYWAY...

I'M GOING TO DEVOTE THE REST OF MY LIFE TO MAKING MY DOG HAPPY..

NO, MA'AM, I HAVEN'T DISCUSSED THIS YET WITH MY MOTHER AND FATHER...

BUT I TALKED IT OVER WITH MY DOG, AND HE SEEMED TO THINK IT'S A GREAT IDEA..

Panel 1: YES, SIR, MR. PRINCIPAL.. I'M GOING TO GIVE UP SCHOOL..EVERYBODY SAYS I'M STUPID ANYWAY...

Panel 2: I'VE DECIDED TO DEVOTE THE REST OF MY LIFE TO MAKING MY DOG HAPPY..

Panel 3: NO, IT ISN'T SUCH A BAD IDEA, IS IT, SIR?

Panel 4: WELL, MAYBE YOU SHOULD TALK IT OVER WITH YOUR CAT, AND SEE WHAT HE THINKS..

Panel 5: REALLY? JUST FROM WHAT I SAID TO HIM? I CAN'T BELIEVE IT!

Panel 6: GUESS WHAT..OUR SCHOOL PRINCIPAL HAS RESIGNED!

Panel 7: HE'S GOING TO DEVOTE THE REST OF HIS LIFE TO MAKING HIS CAT HAPPY..

Panel 8: NO, MA'AM, I'VE NEVER TALKED TO A COUNSELOR BEFORE..

Panel 9: WELL, I'VE ALWAYS BEEN SORT OF A USELESS PERSON SO I THOUGHT I'D JUST DEVOTE THE REST OF MY LIFE TO MAKING MY DOG HAPPY...

Panel 10: I SUPPOSE YOU THINK I'M CRAZY..

Panel 11: REALLY? WHAT KIND OF A MONKEY DO YOU HAVE?

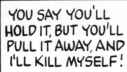

NO, MY BROTHER ISN'T HERE.. HE WENT TO THE MALL...

I THINK HE'S TRYING TO DO THINGS THAT WILL MAKE HIS STUPID DOG HAPPY..

BUNNIES! OOOH, I LOVE LOOKING AT THE BUNNIES!

PET SHOP

HEY, CHUCK, WHAT'S THIS ABOUT YOU QUITTING SCHOOL SO YOU CAN DEVOTE YOUR LIFE TO MAKING YOUR DOG HAPPY?

ASK HIM IF HE STILL LOVES ME

MARCIE WANTS TO KNOW WHY YOU DON'T DEVOTE YOUR LIFE TO MAKING HER HAPPY?

THAT'S NOT WHAT I SAID, SIR!

YEAH, WELL, SHE'S WEIRD, CHUCK..

HERE, HAVE ANOTHER COOKIE...

WE HAD A GOOD TIME TODAY, DIDN'T WE? HAVE I MADE YOU HAPPY?

I'D SAY I'M ABOUT ONE COOKIE AWAY FROM BEING HAPPY..

WE HAD A GOOD TIME AGAIN TODAY DIDN'T WE?

WE SURE DID..

IS THERE ANYTHING YOU'D LIKE TO DO TOMORROW?

MAYBE WE COULD TRY SOMETHING DIFFERENT..

TOMORROW LET'S HAVE THE JELLY DOUGHNUTS BEFORE THE PIZZA..

IT'S OUR NEW SCHOOL PRINCIPAL..HE SAYS YOU SHOULD COME BACK TO SCHOOL...

YES, SIR ..I'LL BE BACK TOMORROW..I'VE BEEN STAYING HOME TO MAKE MY DOG HAPPY...

WELL, HE ATE A LOT OF COOKIES AND STUFF YESTERDAY..

I THINK I HAPPIED HIM TO THE VET..

YES, SIR, IT'S GOOD TO BE BACK IN SCHOOL AGAIN.. I TRIED TO MAKE MY DOG HAPPY, BUT ALL I DID WAS MAKE HIM SICK...

YOU HAVEN'T MET MY DOG, HAVE YOU, SIR?

SNOOPY, THIS IS OUR NEW PRINCIPAL..

IT'D BE NICE, SIR, IF YOU RETURNED HIS SALUTE..

37

Cooking Hints

When mixing dog food in a bowl, the water can either be put in first or added last.

Who cares?

YES, MA'AM.. I LEARNED A LOT TODAY...JUST BEING HERE WAS WORTH THE PRICE OF ADMISSION...

OF COURSE, I DIDN'T PAY ANYTHING!

HA HA HA HA HA HA!

YES, MA'AM

YOU'RE WEIRD, SIR..

WAKE ME WHEN THE SCHOOL BUS COMES..

HERE IT COMES NOW... IT'S ALMOST TO THE MIDDLE OF THE BLOCK..

YOU WOKE ME TOO SOON.. I COULD HAVE SLEPT ANOTHER THIRTY FEET...

UGH, MARCIE! HOW CAN YOU EAT THAT?

IT'S NOT NICE, SIR, TO MAKE DISPARAGING REMARKS ABOUT WHAT SOMEONE IS EATING!

ACTUALLY, IF YOU CAN'T SAY SOMETHING NICE, YOU SHOULDN'T SAY ANYTHING AT ALL...

YOU HAVE A CUTE LUNCH, MARCIE..

THE TEACHER SAID I COULD BRING YOU TO SCHOOL FOR A DAY.. SHE SAID THE OTHER KIDS MIGHT ENJOY IT...

BUT WHY DO YOU HAVE TO OVERDO EVERYTHING?

WHEN YOU LIVE ALONE IN THE DESERT, NO ONE INVITES YOU OVER FOR THANKSGIVING..

YOU HAVE TO PRETEND YOU'RE HAVING YOUR OWN TURKEY DINNER ...

NO MATTER HOW HARD YOU PRETEND, A ROCK IS STILL A ROCK..

I WENT INTO A STORE YESTERDAY TO TRY ON A PATHETIC HELMET...

THE CLERK SAID, "YOU MUST MEAN A 'PITH' HELMET"

AFTER I PUT ONE ON, HE SAID, "MAYBE YOU WERE RIGHT.."

"ON YOU IT LOOKS PATHETIC!"

IF YOU WEAR A PITH HELMET IN THE DESERT, YOU LOOK LIKE A LEADER..

EVERYONE TREATS YOU WITH MORE RESPECT

I THINK

NO, MA'AM...AS THE SAYING GOES, LET'S NOT "GILD THE LILY"

ACTUALLY, SIR, THE CORRECT PHRASE IS "PAINT THE LILY"

AIRBRUSH, VARNISH, SPRAY PAINT...WHO CARES?

I KNOW THE ANSWER, MA'AM.. I JUST CAN'T THINK.. BUT I KNOW THE ANSWER.. I KNOW IT...

IT'S RIGHT ON THE TIP OF MY TONGUE..

CAN YOU MAKE IT OUT FROM THERE?

THE WORLD WAR I FLYING ACE LOOKS LONELY..

PERHAPS ANOTHER ROOT BEER WOULD HELP TO CURE HIS LONELINESS...

I DOUBT IT..

HAVE I EVER TOLD THE WORLD WAR I FLYING ACE HOW MUCH I ADMIRE HIS BEAUTIFUL SILK SCARF?

PERHAPS THE FLYING ACE MIGHT BE WILLING TO TRADE IT FOR A LITTLE KISS...

SEE THOSE TRAFFIC SIGNALS? EACH ONE COST MORE THAN A THOUSAND DOLLARS

THE FOUR POLES COST NINE THOUSAND DOLLARS..

THE WHOLE CORNER, LIGHTS, POLES, WIRING, LABOR..COST SIXTY THOUSAND DOLLARS

SO I TAKE SIX STEPS, AND THE "WALK" SIGN GOES OFF!

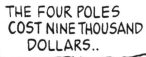

I DON'T THINK YOU'RE THE REAL SANTA CLAUS..

IF YOU'RE THE REAL SANTA, WHERE ARE YOUR HELPERS?

HELP HELP HELP

THAT'S THE DUMBEST THING I'VE EVER SEEN!

WHO CARES? MERRY CHRISTMAS, SWEETIE! WOOF, WOOF, WOOF!

FOR ME? THANK YOU VERY MUCH

"FOR THE ROUND-HEADED KID.. MERRY CHRISTMAS"

IT WOULD BE NICE TO HAVE A DOG WHO REMEMBERED YOUR NAME

56

WHY DO I HAVE THE FEELING THAT SOMEONE HAS JUST THROWN A SNOWBALL AT ME?

IF THAT SNOWBALL HITS ME, THE PERSON WHO THREW IT IS GOING TO REGRET IT FOR THE REST OF HIS LIFE!

SMART! VERY, VERY SMART!

THAT MAKES ME MAD! NEW YEAR'S WAS MY IDEA, AND NOW EVERYBODY'S COPYING IT!

I NEVER REALIZED IT WAS YOUR IDEA

SURE, NO ONE EVER HEARD OF IT UNTIL I CAME ALONG..

ACTUALLY, I THOUGHT OF THANKSGIVING, TOO, BUT I'VE NEVER SAID ANYTHING..

I'M CURIOUS AS TO WHY YOU'RE SITTING WAY BACK HERE..

IF IT'S A BIG ONE, AND I HAVE TO RUN, I WANT A GOOD HEAD START...

MY NAME IS LYDIA, BUT FOR TODAY YOU CAN CALL ME "SNOWFLAKE"

YOU CAN CALL ME "SNOWFLAKE" BECAUSE THERE'S ONLY ONE OF ME IN THE WHOLE WORLD!

I'LL HAVE TO GET BACK TO YOU ON THAT..

WHAT WOULD YOU DO IF I TOLD YOU THIS WOULD BE A GOOD TIME FOR YOU TO GIVE UP THAT STUPID BLANKET?

I'D PROBABLY IGNORE YOU, AND PUT THE BLANKET OVER MY HEAD

WHAT WOULD YOU DO IF I TOLD YOU THIS WOULD BE A GOOD TIME TO STOP BEING SO CRABBY?

IS THIS THE TOUR BUS TO STONEHENGE?

NO, THIS IS THE REGULAR SCHOOL BUS THAT GOES TO PINECREST ELEMENTARY SCHOOL EVERY DAY OF YOUR LIFE...

HOW DID I GET ON THE WRONG BUS?

SHOVEL YOUR WALK?

I'M TRYING TO SAVE UP MONEY FOR COLLEGE...

MY BADMINTON SCHOLARSHIP FELL THROUGH..

I WASN'T SURE I HEARD A DOUGHNUT CALLING ME...

BUT THEN I SAW A LUNCH BOX WALK BY..

SCHULZ

I HEARD THE TEACHER, SIR.. SHE SAID YOUR REPORT SOUNDED LIKE YOU WROTE IT ON THE SCHOOL BUS...

I WAS FLATTERED, MARCIE...

ACTUALLY, I WROTE IT AFTER I GOT OFF THE BUS, AND WAS WALKING UP THE STAIRS INTO SCHOOL..

HERE'S THE FIERCE SNOW SNAKE SNEAKING UP ON A VICTIM...

JUST THE OTHER DAY I WAS READING THAT THERE ISN'T SUCH A THING AS A SNOW SNAKE...

IT'S TOO COLD TO GO TO SCHOOL TODAY...

TELL THE TEACHER TO BRING THE CLASS HERE TO MY ROOM, AND I'LL JUST STAY UNDER THE COVERS...

WHERE HAVE YOU BEEN? YOU ALMOST MISSED THE BUS..

I GOT INVOLVED

C'MON, CHUCK..ANSWER THE PHONE

HELLO?

HI, CHUCK..DO YOU HAVE A PENCIL HANDY?

NO, BUT I CAN GET ONE..

WE HAVE A NEW PHONE NUMBER..I JUST WANT TO GIVE IT TO YOU

ASK HIM IF HE STILL LOVES ME

FROM NOW ON THAT'S OUR NUMBER.. DID YOU GET IT?

ASK HIM IF HE EVER THINKS ABOUT ME...

I'M NOT SURE I CAN REMEMBER IT

DIDN'T YOU WRITE IT DOWN? I TOLD YOU TO GET A PENCIL...

I DON'T HAVE ANY PAPER..YOU DIDN'T SAY ANYTHING ABOUT PAPER...

CHUCK, YOU BLOCK-HEAD!

ASK HIM IF HE STILL THINKS I'M CUTE...

FORGET IT, CHUCK! DON'T CALL ME..I'LL CALL YOU... LIKE IN A HUNDRED YEARS!

YOU DIDN'T ASK HIM

 I WONDER WHAT I CAN DO TO MAKE THAT LITTLE RED-HAIRED GIRL NOTICE ME..

 MAYBE IF I WALK AROUND THE ROOM A BIT... I'LL BET SHE NOTICES ME NOW...

 ESPECIALLY AFTER I GET MY SLEEVE CAUGHT IN THE PENCIL SHARPENER..

 IF THAT LITTLE RED-HAIRED GIRL SEES ME STANDING HERE WITH MY SLEEVE CAUGHT IN THE PENCIL SHARPENER, SHE'LL THINK I'M THE DUMBEST PERSON IN THE WORLD

 WHAT I HAVE TO DO IS WRIGGLE OUT OF MY SWEATER BUT STILL LOOK REAL COOL...

YES, MA'AM, I'D LIKE PERMISSION TO LEAVE EARLY..MY DOG IS EXPECTING ME HOME

SOMETIMES HE HAS BAD DREAMS AND NEEDS COMFORTING...

WHAT DID SHE SAY, CHARLIE BROWN?

WELL, SHE STARTED OFF BY SAYING SOMETHING ABOUT "IN ALL HER YEARS OF TEACHING," AND THEN I MISSED THE LAST PART...

DOG BREAK!

YES, MA'AM..A "DOG BREAK" IS WHEN YOU GET TO GO HOME TO SEE IF YOUR DOG MISSES YOU OR NEEDS YOU FOR ANYTHING...

NICE TRY..

YOU'RE RIGHT.. WE SHOULD HAVE HAD A PICTURE OF THAT..

YOUR NEW HAIRDO IS SORT OF IN MY FACE, SIR...

I CAN'T HEAR YOU, MA'AM.. THERE'S AN ECHO IN HERE...

SO WE'RE RIDING ALONG IN THE CAR, SEE...

JUST AS WE COME TO A STOPLIGHT, A PICKUP TRUCK PULLS ALONGSIDE WITH A BIG DOG IN THE BACK...

THE STUPID DOG BARKED AT ME!

I WAS OFFENDED

Dear Grandma, Sorry it has taken me so long to thank you for the Christmas present.

But better late than never, huh? Ha Ha Ha Ha

WHAT DO YOU THINK?

I'M NOT SURE..

I'LL ADD ANOTHER "HA"

GRAMMA IS MAD AT ME...

SHE SAID IT'S INEXCUSABLE TO BE SIX WEEKS LATE WITH A "THANK YOU" NOTE

I DIDN'T THINK SIX WEEKS WAS THAT LONG TO A GRANDMOTHER..

DOES A GRAMMA HAVE THE RIGHT TO CRITICIZE A GRANDCHILD, OR SHOULD SHE CRITICIZE THE KID'S MOTHER WHO, OF COURSE, IS HER OWN CHILD?

IN MY OPINION, I DON'T THINK SHE DOES, AND I THINK I'M GOING TO TELL HER...

UNLESS, OF COURSE, YOU WANT TO..

HELLO, GRAMMA? I JUST CALLED TO APOLOGIZE..YOU WERE RIGHT..I SHOULD HAVE WRITTEN MY "THANK YOU" NOTE SOONER..

YOU WERE RIGHT..YES, YOU TAUGHT ME A VALUABLE LESSON..THANK YOU, GRAMMA..

IT'S EASY TO APOLOGIZE TO AN ANSWERING MACHINE

EACH FAMILY HAS A CHAIN OF COMMAND, AND DO YOU KNOW WHO'S THE LOWEST ON THAT CHAIN? GUESS!

IT'S THE DOG! THE DOG IS THE LOWEST! DO YOU UNDERSTAND THAT?

I SAID, DO YOU UNDERSTAND THAT?

THEY HATE IT WHEN YOU JUST STARE AT 'EM LIKE THIS..

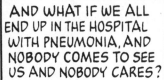

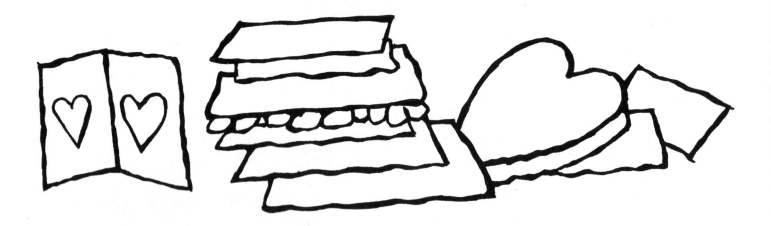

THIS IS MY REPORT ON HOW TO LIVE..

THEY SAY THE BEST WAY IS JUST TO LIVE ONE DAY AT A TIME..

IF YOU TRY TO LIVE SEVEN DAYS AT A TIME, THE WEEK WILL BE OVER BEFORE YOU KNOW IT..

MY GRAMPA SAYS THAT WHEN HE WAS SMALL, AND GOT SICK, THE DOCTOR GAVE HIM BABY ASPIRIN...

LAST WEEK HIS CARDIOLOGIST TOLD HIM HE SHOULD TAKE ONE BABY ASPIRIN EVERY DAY...

GRAMPA SAYS THAT SOMEHOW HE HAS THE FEELING HE'S NOT GETTING ANYPLACE..

YOU HAVEN'T CALLED US IN A LONG WHILE, CHUCK..DON'T YOU LIKE US ANYMORE?

OR MAYBE YOU NEVER DID LIKE US..IS THAT TRUE, CHUCK? THAT YOU NEVER DID LIKE US? HUH, CHUCK? HUH?

WE'RE SORRY..THE NUMBER YOU HAVE CALLED IS NO LONGER IN SERVICE..IT WAS A MINUTE AGO, BUT THESE THINGS HAPPEN..

THIS IS MY REPORT ON THE WIND...

WIND BLOWS YOUR HAIR AROUND WHEN YOU'RE WALKING TO SCHOOL, AND AFTER YOU GET THERE, YOU DON'T HAVE A COMB..

IT ALSO GIVES YOU SOMETHING TO WRITE ABOUT WHEN YOU CAN'T THINK OF ANYTHING ELSE, AND YOU CAN'T SEE WHAT YOU'RE READING...

88

It was a dark and stormy night.

So what else is new?

YOUR STORIES AREN'T ROMANTIC ENOUGH

TRY TO MAKE THEM MORE ROMANTIC..

When he said, "I love you," it was a dark and stormy night.

Dear Contributor, We are returning your dumb story

Note that we have not included our return address.

We have moved to a new office,

and we don't want you to know where we are.

THESE ARE THE STATISTICS FOR OUR BASEBALL TEAM LAST YEAR, CHARLIE BROWN...

ACCORDING TO THESE FIGURES, OUR TEAM WILL BE EVEN WORSE THIS YEAR THAN IT WAS LAST YEAR..

I WONDER IF IT'S POSSIBLE TO HAVE AN ENTIRE SEASON RAINED OUT..

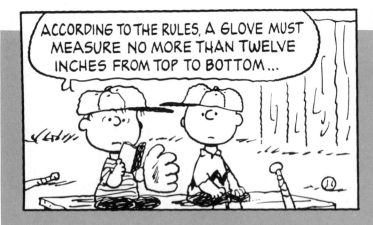
ACCORDING TO THE RULES, A GLOVE MUST MEASURE NO MORE THAN TWELVE INCHES FROM TOP TO BOTTOM...

WE HAVE A LEFT-FIELDER WHO ISN'T THAT TALL..

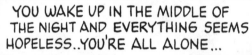

I'VE OFTEN WONDERED WHY YOU DECIDED TO BECOME A CACTUS WHEN YOU MIGHT HAVE BEEN AN ORANGE TREE..

NO, THAT'S ALL RIGHT..

I CAN UNDERSTAND YOUR NOT WANTING TO DISCUSS IT..

DOES YOUR GRAMPA PLAY MUCH GOLF THESE DAYS?

HE SAYS HE PLAYS MOSTLY IN HIS HEAD...

BUT HE SAYS THE COURSE IS TOO NARROW..

FLAG MAN AHEAD

I COULDN'T SLEEP LAST NIGHT.. I KEPT WORRYING ABOUT SCHOOL, AND ABOUT LIFE AND ABOUT EVERYTHING..

I DIDN'T SLEEP WELL, EITHER...

ALL NIGHT LONG I KEPT WORRYING THAT THE MOON WAS GOING TO FALL ON MY HEAD..

AND SOMETIMES WHEN A RABBIT IS FRIGHTENED, IT WILL SIT VERY STILL LIKE THIS SO NO ONE WILL SEE IT...

OF COURSE, YOU CAN STILL SEE ME! I WAS JUST GIVING YOU AN EXAMPLE!!

YOU CAN'T EXPLAIN ANYTHING TO A BIRD!

ARE THEY AT IT AGAIN?

WHY NOT?

WHAT DO THEY HAVE TO LOSE?

ONE OF THESE TIMES I THINK THEY'RE GONNA MAKE IT..

ONE SENIOR CITIZEN, PLEASE..

THAT'S RIGHT.. IT'S YOUR JOB TO TELL EVERYONE THAT SPRING HAS COME..

BUT NOT IN DETAIL!

"AFTERNOON DOG BREAK"!

YES, MA'AM, FOR "AFTERNOON DOG BREAK" THE OWNER RUSHES HOME, GIVES HIS DOG A SNACK, HOLDS HIM IN HIS LAP AND PETS HIM FOR TEN MINUTES...

YOU'RE RIGHT, MA'AM.. IT'S VERY SIMILAR TO "MORNING DOG BREAK"

105

I'M AWAKE!

YES, MA'AM. WELL, THAT MIGHT BE HARD TO ANSWER..

I MEAN, IT WOULD BE COMPARING APPLES AND EGGS..

ORANGES

YES, ORANGES AND EGGS...

APPLES AND ORANGES...

OR EGGS AND PUMPKINS!

PUMPKINS AND CELERY!

CARROTS AND COCONUTS!

GRAPES AND CUCUMBERS!

BANANAS AND RADISHES!

YES, MA'AM

YOU'RE WEIRD, SIR, BUT YOU'RE A LOT OF FUN

PRINCIPAL'S OFFICE

FRED IS LONELY AND WANTS TO GO HOME?

EVERYONE IN THE WORLD IS LONELY, FRED..JUST GO TO SLEEP...

TRY TO THINK OF SOMETHING NICE...

I AGREE.. A HOT FUDGE SUNDAE WOULD TASTE GOOD RIGHT NOW..

WELL, IT WAS A GREAT HIKE, MEN..LET'S DO IT AGAIN SOON...

BETTER TAKE CARE OF THAT SORE THROAT, BILL!

 WELL, MA'AM, I DIDN'T HAVE ANY WRITING PAPER...

 SO I DID MY HOMEWORK ON A PAPER PLATE..

 DIDN'T CARE FOR IT, HUH, MA'AM?

 I'M WAITING FOR A SCHOOL BUS THAT WILL TAKE ME TO SCHOOL..AND FOR WHAT?

 TO GET ON ANOTHER BUS, AND GO ON A FIELD TRIP TO SOME STUPID PLACE I'VE NEVER HEARD OF! I CAN'T STAND IT!

 I SHOULD HAVE STAYED IN PRE-SCHOOL..

 WHY ARE WE GOING ON A FIELD TRIP WHEN IT'S GOING TO RAIN?

 WHAT MAKES YOU THINK IT'S GOING TO RAIN? OUR TEACHER SAID IT'S GOING TO BE A NICE DAY...

 FIELD TRIPS CAUSE RAIN..

MAKE WAY FOR THE KING OF THE JUNGLE!

I ALWAYS THOUGHT THE LION WAS THE KING OF THE JUNGLE...

MAKE WAY FOR THE NEW IMPROVED KING OF THE JUNGLE!

SO I FIGURED IF YOU'RE GOING TO BE KING OF THE JUNGLE, YOU SHOULD HAVE A THRONE.. AND I THINK I'VE FOUND ONE

IF SOMEONE COMES ALONG TO WAIT FOR A BUS, YOU MAY HAVE TO MOVE OVER A LITTLE BIT..

113

SO I ASK MYSELF WHAT COULD BE MORE STUPID THAN STANDING OUT HERE IN RIGHT FIELD IN THE RAIN?

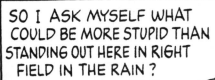

I KEEP ASKING MYSELF THE SAME QUESTION OVER AND OVER.. WHAT COULD BE MORE STUPID? THEN I ASK MYSELF AGAIN...

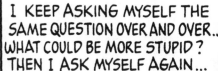

IN THE MEANTIME, I'M GETTING WET..

I DON'T BELIEVE IT..YOU'VE BEEN SELECTED FOR JURY DUTY!

THIS IS RIDICULOUS! DON'T THEY KNOW YOU'RE A DOG?

WHAT'S WRONG WITH THAT?

OBVIOUSLY, THERE'S BEEN A MISTAKE..

I'LL GO IF THEY GIVE AWAY FREE COOKIES..

WHAT WE'RE LOOKING FOR IS THE JURY ASSEMBLY ROOM ON THE SECOND FLOOR...

I SORT OF WISH YOU HADN'T WORN THAT OUTFIT...

YOU GET MORE RESPECT IF THEY KNOW YOU SERVED HONORABLY IN WORLD WAR I

YES, MA'AM, THIS IS MY DOG.. HE WAS TOLD TO REPORT HERE THIS MORNING FOR JURY DUTY

WHY IS HE WEARING GOGGLES?

PLEASE, MA'AM, DON'T ASK ME TO TRY TO EXPLAIN THAT..

THE LADY SAID FOR YOU TO SIT HERE UNTIL THEY CALL YOUR NAME...

LOOK AT THIS..IT SAYS IF YOU SERVE ON A JURY, THEY PAY YOU FIVE DOLLARS A DAY..

FIVE DOLLARS WILL BUY A LOT OF COOKIES!

YES, SIR...NO, YOUR HONOR, I'VE NEVER MET A JUDGE BEFORE..

WELL, MY DOG GOT THIS CARD IN THE MAIL SAYING HE HAD BEEN SELECTED FOR JURY DUTY, AND...

THIS IS A NICE ROOM..IT REMINDS ME OF THE TIME I WAS CALLED IN TO ADVISE GENERAL PERSHING...

SO THEN WHAT HAPPENED?

THEN THE JUDGE APOLOGIZED TO US FOR THE MIS-UNDERSTANDING, AND SAID WE WERE GOOD CITIZENS FOR TRYING TO DO WHAT WAS RIGHT..

I WAS ALL SET TO VOTE 'GUILTY'!

THIS IS ALWAYS A DIFFICULT GREEN TO READ...

MAYBE I SHOULD WAIT FOR IT TO COME OUT IN PAPERBACK..

YOU WERE SITTING THERE IN YOUR BOOTH, AND I WAS SITTING RIGHT HERE WHERE I AM NOW...

THE DOCTOR

PSYCHIATRIC HELP 5¢

THE DOCTOR IS IN

AND I REMEMBER WHAT YOU TOLD ME..

YOU SAID THAT WHEN I BECOME DEPRESSED, I SHOULD ALWAYS REMEMBER THAT "EVERY CLOUD HAS A SILVER LINING"

I WANT YOU TO LOOK AT THIS...

HMM..VERY INTERESTING

THE DOCTOR IS IN

I THINK I SEE THE PROBLEM...

HELP 5¢

WHAT WE HAVE HERE IS A DEFECTIVE CLOUD..

THE DOCTOR

WHAT DID ONE GOLFER SAY TO THE OTHER GOLFER? 'READ ANY GOOD GREENS LATELY?'

HAHAHAHA!

CADDIES SHOULDN'T TRY TO BE FUNNY..

WHY WOULD ANYONE WANT TO SAY, "GOOD NIGHT" TO THE MOON?

THERE'S NO HURRY, I GUESS, BUT LET ME KNOW WHEN I CAN HAVE YOUR SUPPER DISH...

THIS IS THE REPORT I'M GIVING TOMORROW ON VOLCANOES...

"LIFE IN THE VILLAGE WAS PEACEFUL UNTIL THE VOLCANO INTERRUPTED"

HOW IMPOLITE

WHAT DID YOU SAY?

I SAID, IT SOUNDS LIKE A GOOD REPORT

I'LL GO READ IT TO YOUR DOG..

I THOUGHT MAYBE I WAS THUMBIDEXTROUS, BUT I GUESS I'M NOT..

I HOPE YOU NOTICED THAT I'VE BROUGHT YOUR SUPPER FIVE MINUTES EARLY TONIGHT

DOGS ARE NOT REQUIRED TO NOTICE THINGS LIKE THAT

LET'S NOT GIVE UP, CHARLIE BROWN..

REMEMBER WHAT THEY SAY.. "THE GAME ISN'T OVER UNTIL THE FAT LADY SINGS"

OR UNTIL THE SHORTSTOP WAKES UP

STRIKE THREE!
RATS!
I CAN'T DO ANYTHING RIGHT..
I SHOULD JUST GO IN THE HOUSE AND STAY THERE FOREVER...
IF I CAN'T DO ANYTHING ELSE, AT LEAST I CAN SIT AND HOLD MY DOG IN MY LAP...
BONK!
SIGH
SCHULZ